AF439360

A Natural Born Leader

Some knew him as the son of a wealthy Virginia tobacco grower, slave owner, and livestock farmer. Some knew him as a young surveyor at the age of 17. Others knew him as a dedicated, intelligent student who mastered the basics of math, geography and English at home as well as in the local church school.

Before his life was over, at the age of 67, those who studied his life knew him as a courageous battlefield commander, a caring and humble statesman, and even a poet! In summary, George Washington was a natural born leader! It was no surprise that he was unanimously elected as our country's first president on April 30th, 1789.

Trivial Fun Fact

George Washington did not have a middle name! Middle names did not become popular in the United States until the early to mid-1800s. The first 5 US presidents did not have middle names. John Quincy Adams, elected in 1826, was our first president with a middle name. Now you know!

George's earliest relative to move to the Americas, great-grandfather John Washington, had moved from England in 1657 to the newly-established British Colony of Virginia.

George was born in 1732 on Ferry Farm, just outside of Fredericksburg, on the banks of the Rappahannock River. George's father, Augustine, lost his first wife, Jane Butler, who had given him 3 children. Young George was the first of 5 additional children born to Augustine and his second wife, Mary

Ball Washington.

George's father Augustin e died when George was only 11, leaving George's older step-brother, Lawrence, to run the family farm. Ferry Farm continued to be wellmanaged and grew to over 1,000 acres by his father's death. George was well-cared for by his older stepbrother, learning the art of civil surveying by the age of 17, when he became professionally employed by Culpeper County, Virginia.

Unfortunately for George, Lawrence passed away from tuberculosis when George was only 20, with the responsibilities of a very large and lucrative farming operation falling firmly on young George's shoulders. He immediately relocated to another tobacco plantation that Lawrence had inherited when his father passed away. This new plantation would later become known as Mt. Vernon. Under George's able management, Mt. Vernon grew quickly to a sizeable estate of 8,000 acres!

"Father, I Can Not Tell a Lie: I Cut the Tree," engraving by John C. McRae, 1867

Trivial Fun Fact

One of the most popular myths told about young George Washington was that he cut down his father's favorite cherry tree at the age of 6, then admitted his error in stating, "I cannot tell a lie", as pictured in the above engraving. The myth can be attributed to author Mason Locke Weems, appearing in Weems' biography, *The Life of Washington*, 5th ed., in 1806. Weems' purpose was to portray Washington as honest and virtuous, although there is no other historical record that the cherry tree incident ever really happened. Now you know!

Historic Plaque at Ferry Farm

War On The Horizon

Not long after relocating to Mt. Vernon, both French and British armed troops had begun to move west from the coast where they had established forts in what is now Pennsylvania and New York states. The year was 1753. George Washington was only 21 years old!

This entire region grew ripe for conflict as French troops tried to gain strategic military advantage, the British government continued to issue land grants for British settlers who were brave enough to attempt to tame the lands to the west. Meanwhile, several native Indian tribes resisted the early beginnings of "Manifest Destiny", Colonial America's compulsion to move even deeper into the untamed wilderness.

Washington had proven himself such a capable farmer and business leader that Virginia's Lieutenant Governor, Robert Dinwiddie, appointed Washington to the position of major in the Virginia colonial militia. George's first major assignment came on October 31, 1753, which was Halloween day.

George was assigned to lead a Virginia Militia platoon to Fort Leboeuf in what is now Northwest Pennsylvania, just 15 miles from Lake Erie. Since this land had been previously claimed by Great Britain, George's assignment was to order French troops to "back off", to abandon the fort immediately. His demands were met with a refusal. Major George Washington and his militiamen then scurried back to Virginia.

Governor Dinwiddie immediately equipped Washington with a fresh supply of troops and ordered him to establish an outpost in the western Pennsylvania territory. In pursuit of his goal, Washington and his men attacked Fort Duquesne which was strategically located at the junction of the Allegheny and Monongahela Rivers, the beginning of the Ohio River and the center of modern day Pittsburgh.

Washington commanded a small force while killing 10 French soldiers at Fort Duquesne, including the fort commander, exhibiting exceptional bravery for a young man of 21! Little did Washington realize, this early battle would lead to the French and Indian War, which pitted French and British troops against each other, while also relying on native American manpower.

Although French troops and their North American colonists numbered about 60,000, the population of British colonists and soldiers was more than 30

times that number at nearly 2 million!
The major catalyst of the French and Indian War, also referred to as the *Seven Years' War* by French and British historians, was a surprise attack by Washington's militiamen upon a French patrol in May of 1754, known as the *Battle of Jumonville Glen*, near to the southwest border of Pennsylvania. Washington was still quite young at just 22 years of age!

It was here that Washington and his troops, along with the aid of a small group of Mingo warriors and their leader, Half King, surrounded a group of 35 Canadian troops under the command of Joseph Coulon de Villiers de Jumonville. Among the dead were 10 French Canadians, including Jumonville, while the remaining French soldiers were taken captive.

Following several months of localized skirmishes, France and England officially declared war on each other in 1756. The French recruited the support of several native American Indian tribes, which included the Lenape, Ojibwa, Algonquin, Wyandot, Shawnee, and Ottawa. Likewise, the British enlisted the aid of the Iroquois, Catawba, Mingo, and Cherokee tribes.

Little did George Washington know at this time, he was in training for a much bigger battle – the American War for Independence that would commence in just a few short years!

French and Indian War Map

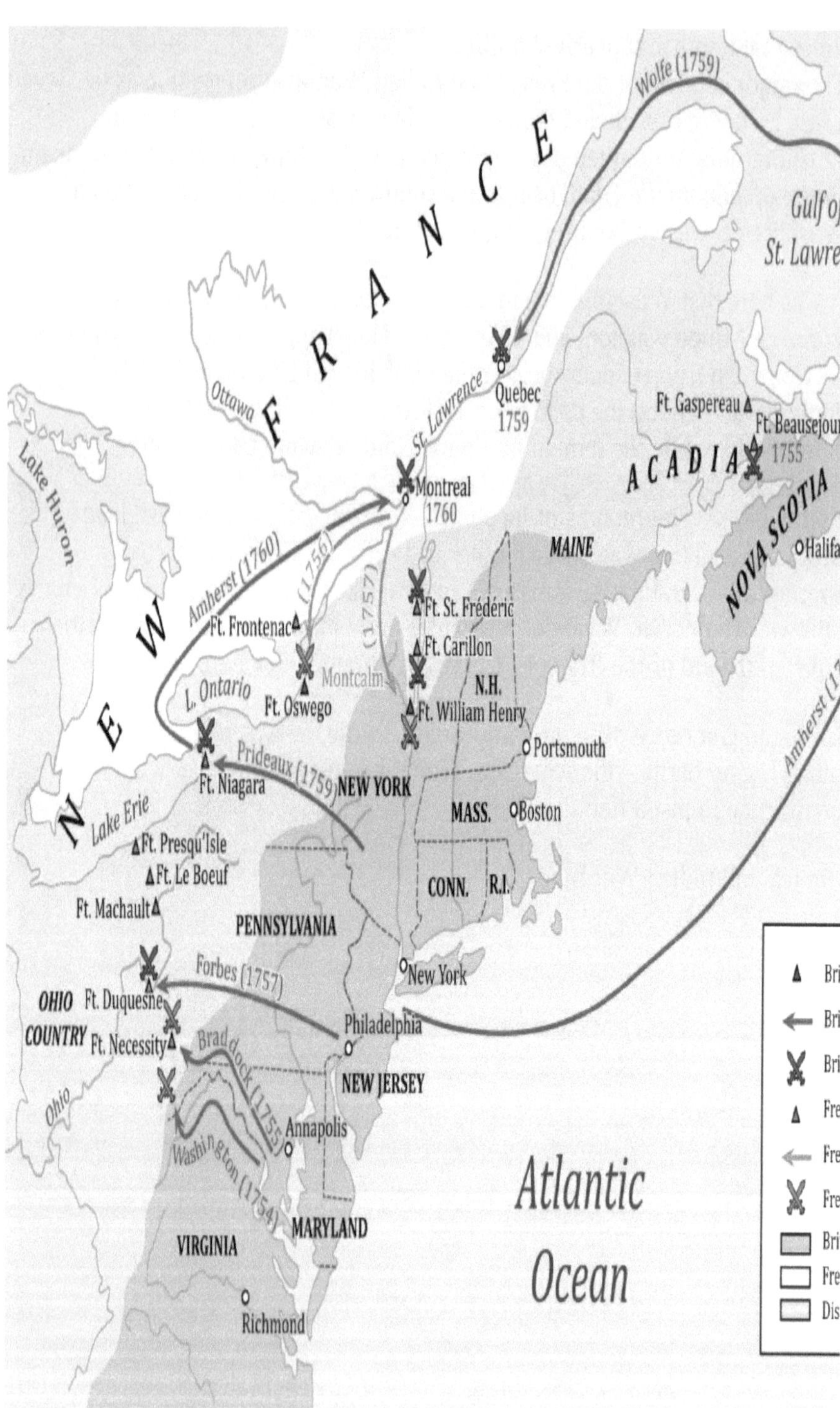

F R A N C E
N E W
Wolfe (1759)
Gulf of
St. Lawren
Lake Huron
Ottawa
St. Lawrence
Quebec
1759
Ft. Gaspereau
Ft. Beausejour
1755
ACADIA
Montreal
1760
NOVA SCOTIA
MAINE
Halifax
Amherst (1760)
(1756)
(1757)
Ft. Frontenac
Ft. St. Frédéric
Ft. Carillon
N.H.
L. Ontario
Montcalm
Ft. Oswego
Ft. William Henry
Prideaux (1759)
NEW YORK
Portsmouth
Ft. Niagara
Amherst (175
Lake Erie
MASS.
Boston
Ft. Presqu'Isle
Ft. Le Boeuf
CONN.
R.I.
Ft. Machault
PENNSYLVANIA
Forbes (1757)
New York
OHIO
Ft. Duquesne
COUNTRY
Ft. Necessity
Philadelphia
Braddock (1755)
NEW JERSEY
Ohio
Washington (1754)
Annapolis
Atlantic
Ocean
MARYLAND
VIRGINIA
Richmond
Bri
Bri
Bri
Fre
Fre
Fre
Bri
Fre
Dis

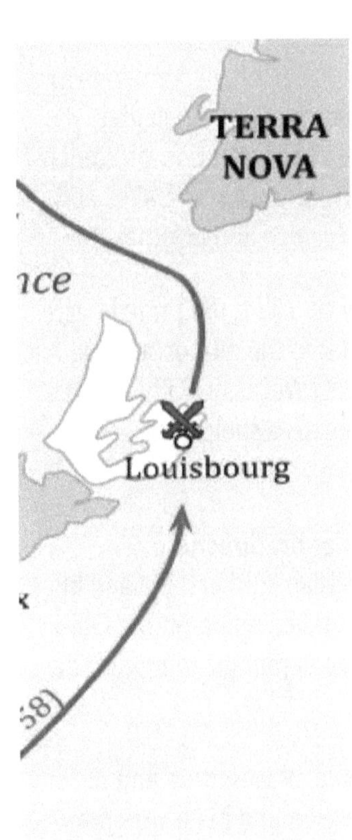

tish fort

tish forces

tish victory

nch fort

nch forces

nch victory

tish possessions

nch possessions

puted areas

Wikipedia

The above map provides a nice picture of the movement of British and French forces from 1754 through 1759. The largest concentration of French settlers was in modern day Canada just to the north of the Great Lakes and the St. Lawrence Seaway, an area known as *New France* at that time.

Shortly after the *Battle of Jumonville Glen* in May of 1774, the French were able to regroup and drive Washington's troops back to the outpost that he had created, first known as *Great Meadows*, later as *Fort Necessity*. This under-sized, inadequate "fort" was little more than a protective shelter for ammunition and supplies.

It was now June of 1774, and Washington had under his direction approximately 300 colonial militiamen and 100 British soldiers. He and his men attempted to establish a more advanced base and crossing on the Ohio River to their west. Meanwhile, French troops were in pursuit following the killing of Jumonville just one month earlier.

After a full day attack on July 3rd, the French forced Washington and his limited forces to surrender Fort Necessity. Washington and his troops were released and freed to return to Williamsburg on July 4, 1754. The French then burned the small fort.

Trivial Fun Fact

It was a myth that Washington had wooden teeth. Although he did have trouble with his teeth most of his adult life, the false teeth shown on the opposite page were made from ivory, lead, and gold. Now you know!

Surviving Set of Washington's Dentures

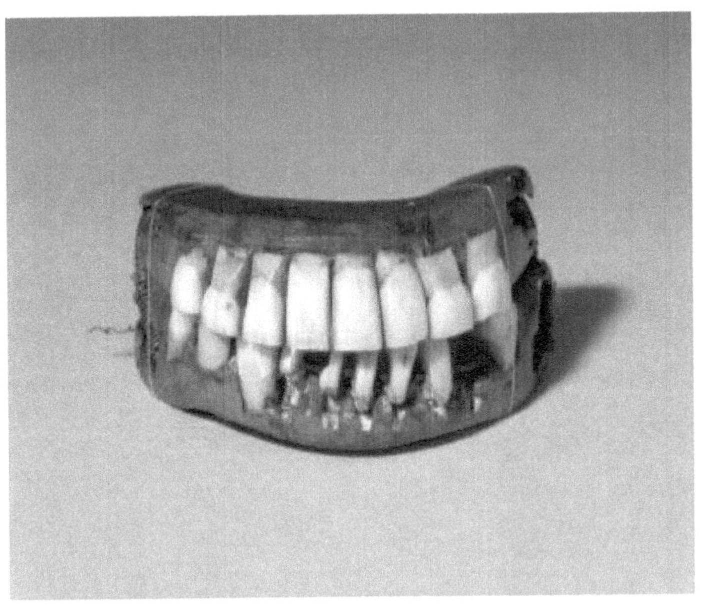

After his surrender at Fort Necessity and his return to Williamsburg, Washington joined British General Edward Braddock who had just arrived from Great Britain. He was given the honorary rank of colonel. Their joint mission was to carry out attacks on the French at Fort Duquesne, Fort Niagara, and Fort St. Frederic at Crown Point, New York.

Not only did their military campaigns result in failure, but General Braddock, while advancing toward Fort Duquesne, was mortally wounded in the *Battle of the Monongahela* on July 9th, 1755, just 10 miles to the east of present day Pittsburgh. Washington barely escaped death himself, taking four bullets through his cloak while suffering the loss of two horses.
Historians report that the *Battle of Monongahela* had been won by a combined French force of 850 soldiers, consisting of 146 Canadian militiamen, 108 French marines and over 600 native American Indians!

General Braddock and Washington, on the other hand, after many days and miles of crossing rough terrain, concluded that Fort Duquesne could be easily overtaken. But once they crossed the Monongahela River with a light infantry force of 1,300, the BritishAmerican militia was ambushed by a much fresher French-Indian force that won the day!

A 19th Century engraving of General Edward Braddock's death at the *Battle of Monongahela* on July 9th, 1755.

Wikipedia

Later that same year, in August of 1755, Washington was named commander of all of Virginia's troops. Amazingly, he was only 23 years old! For the next two years Washington and a rag-tag group of 700 militiamen patrolled Virginia territory's 400 mile-long western border. Toward the end of 1757, Washington fell ill with dysentery and returned to Williamsburg.

After a recovery of a few months, Washington and his troops were directed once again to attempt the capture of the strategically located Fort Duquesne. Although 26 of Washington's men died by friendly fire in this second attack, British troops finally gained control of the Ohio Valley in a major victory over the occupying FrenchIndian forces.

As commander of the entire Virginia militia, Washington's experience had been increasingly frustrating due to slow decision-making, a general lack of support from the Virginia colonial legislature, and poorly trained militiamen.

Washington then applied to become a commissioned officer with the British army. When his application was denied, he resigned his commission in the Virginia militia. He returned to Mt. Vernon, somewhat disillusioned, in December of 1758.

Washington Settles Down and Marries

Just one month following his exit from the French - Indian - British conflict, Washington married Martha Dandridge Custis, a wealthy widow in her own right. Martha and her first husband had built an estate of over 18,000 acres! With additional land that George had earned through his military service, he and wife Martha were now among the wealthiest of Virginia landowners.

Martha also brought son Jacky (age 6) and daughter Patsy (age 4) into the marriage. Patsy would die a few years later, as the country moved into the Revolutionary War. Jacky died after the war was under way, leaving two of his children to be raised by George and Martha.

For the next 10 years, Washington returned to the relatively normal life of a gentleman farmer, a very wealthy farmer at that! He devoted much time to managing his assets and his very large plantation, which employed over 100 slaves. Although Washington disliked that slavery separated families, he accepted that the common practice was the law of the South at that time. He often worked alongside his laborers, maintaining his cattle and horses, working the orchards, and rotating crops, while enjoying fox hunting, fishing, and English style square dancing known as cotillions. Washington had been elected to the Virginia House of Burgesses (colonial legislature) shortly after returning to Mt. Vernon in 1758 and remained sensitive to the growing British occupation and control in the new American colonies, although he did not take a leadership role in the British resistance movement until the passage of the Townshend Acts in 1767.

The French and Indian War had ended in 1763, with the British experiencing serious financial drain on their resources in colonial America. In an effort to raise revenue to pay the mounting salaries of British judges and governors in the colonies, Charles Townshend, a British legislator from the Whig party authored 5 major pieces of legislation designed to place a hefty tax burden on American colonists.

This collection of legislative measures placed taxes on glass, lead, paper, paints, and tea. Resistance slowly mounted following the passage of the Townshend Acts, resulting in protest and a steep decline in the import of British goods.

Washington's first official action in response to "taxation without representation" was to introduce a resolution to the Virginia House of Burgesses which called for a complete boycott of British goods into Boston Harbor as well as the other colonies.

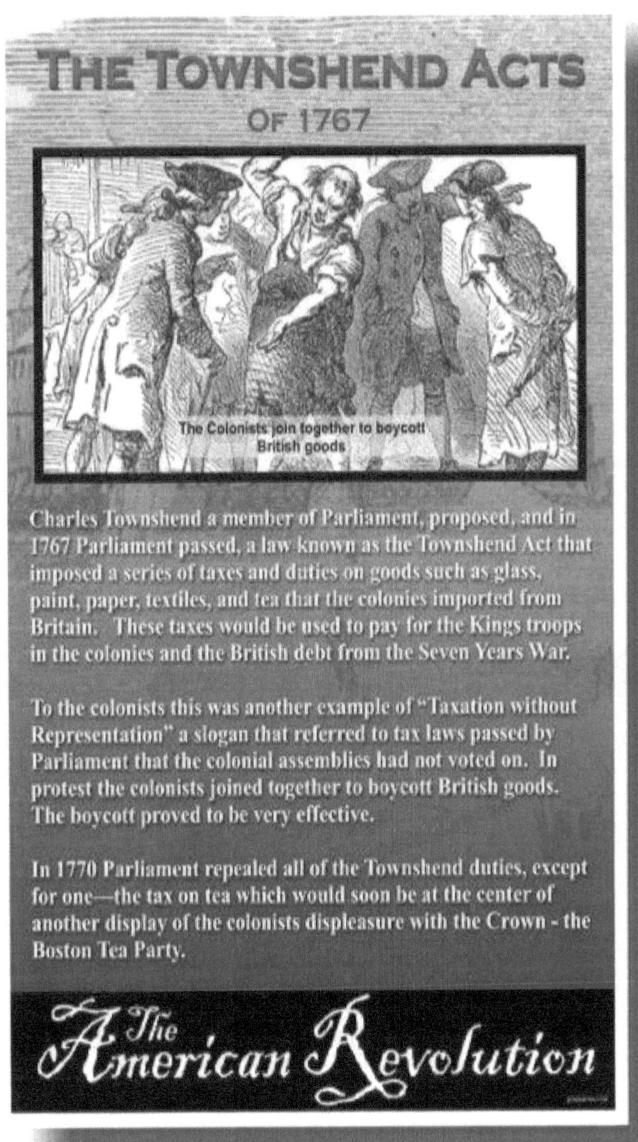

The British Parliament responded with a repeal process under Frederick Lord North which was nearly complete by 1770. The British chose to leave in place, however, the tea tax to continue to demonstrate Parliament's sovereign authority over the colonies, who had no representation in the British

Parliament. This decision was reinforced by the Tea Act of 1773.

On December 3, 1773, a colonial protest group known as the *Sons of Liberty*, staged the *Boston Tea Party* to enact revenge on British rule in defiance of the Tea Act passed earlier that year. An entire shipment of 342 chests of tea shipped by the *East India Company* was dumped into the harbor by colonial protestors dressed at native American Indians! The tea party would prove to be the culmination of the colonial protest movement, ultimately resulting in a full blown armed revolution.

Trivial Fun Fact

To drive the point home, Boston patriots conducted a second *Tea Party* on March 7, 1774, dumping a total of 16 chests into Boston Harbor! The estimated value of tea dumped into the harbor in both incidents was about $1.7 million in today's money! Now you know!

A Second Call to Action

The British Parliament responded to the Boston Tea Parties with the passage of the *Intolerable Acts of 1774*, clearly meant to punish Massachusetts' colonists by further denying them self-governance. Washington chaired a meeting calling for the formation of a Continental Congress in Philadelphia in September of 1774, in which legislation was passed known as the *Fairfax Resolves*. This bold document stated that armed resistance would be used as a last resort to ongoing British tyranny. The British government officially declared Massachusetts to be in a state of rebellion in February of 1775.

In March of 1775, George Washington was selected as a delegate to the First Continental Congress. This small body of 55 met briefly to consider further

boycott of British goods and a list of grievances and rights to present to King Richard III. Those present included John Adams, Samuel Adams, George Washington and Patrick Henry. Their collective concerns fell on deaf ears in England, resulting in the immediate call for a Second Continental Congress, which convened in May of 1775 with 56 delegates from 13 colonies.
Of those present at the Second Congress were many now-famous American patriots, including Ben Franklin, John Hancock, and Thomas Jefferson. After several uncoordinated efforts to seize small local arsenals, drive out local British officials, and to torment British troops in Boston, this group of angry and anxious patriots, in June of 1775, voted to form the new Continental Army. This force consisted of several colonial militias, led by none other than Commanding General, George Washington! One month later, on July 6th, 1775, the Second Congress passed a *Declaration of Causes* which explained the group's rationale for taking up arms in the colonies. It would be two years later that the Congress would declare its independence from Great Britain, on July 4, 1776.

The *Battles of Lexington and Concord*, had already occurred on April 19th, 1775, marking the first armed conflicts of the Revolutionary War. Both battles were fought just outside of Boston in Middlesex County. A British army battalion of 700, under secret orders, attempted to capture a Massachusetts militia supplies depot at Concord. Through intelligence gathering of their own, and warnings spread by several riders including Paul Revere and Samuel Prescott, the Patriots were ready!
With notice of the attack known weeks ahead, the colonials were able to relocate their supplies just prior to the morning of the attack. As the sun rose on Lexington, the first shots fired by the British claimed 8 militiamen. After fighting off the colonial militia, British troops marched on to Concord where they broke into smaller companies in search of hidden supplies.

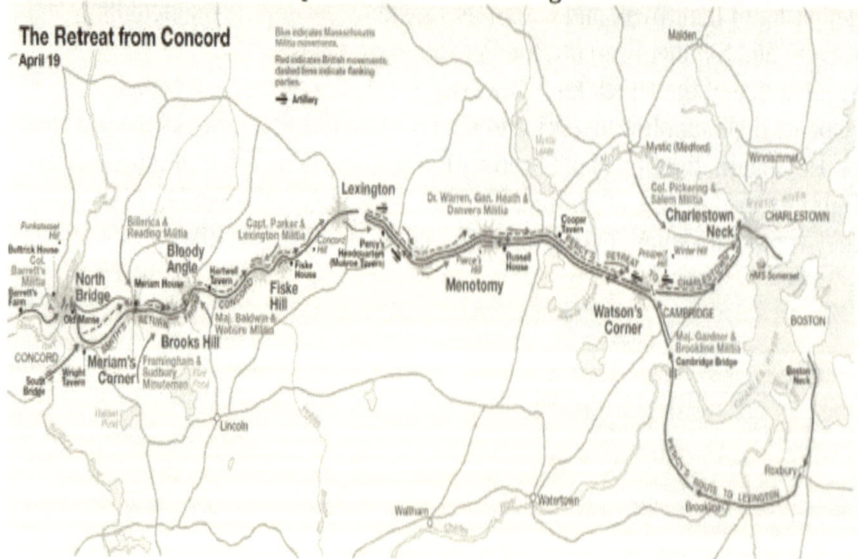

Paul Revere by Pinterest.com

National Parks Service Map The Battles of Lexington and Concord

It was near Concord, at North Bridge, that 400 militiamen held off British troops, driving them back to the main body of their troops in Concord. Both sides suffered casualties as the retreating British fell under constant attack from new militia who had arrived later on the scene.

A combined force of 1,700 British soldiers were forced back to Charlestown, just north of Boston, where militiamen blockaded the narrow land routes to Charlestown and Boston Harbor. The colonial army continued to exercise control of the access in and out of the harbor for the next 11 months as other battles ensued. This blockade by the colonial army is referred to as the *Siege of Boston*.

Seven months following the *Battles of Lexington and Concord*, in November of 1775, Commander George Washington assigned a 25 year-old former book seller, a soldier named Henry Knox, to move several cannons that had been looted from the British fort in northern New York following the *Battle of Fort Ticonderoga* in May of that year.

It was at Ticonderoga, on May 10th, 1775, that Colonel Benedict Arnold along with Colonel Ethan Allen's *Green Mountain Boys*, surprised a group of 12 sleeping British soldiers and easily overcome the fort and its valuable munitions. Arnold and Allen had assembled a militia of 400 men who captured over 100 cannons without injury. It was said that only one shot was fired.

Knox and his recruits performed beautifully in returning the cannons to the Boston area in January of 1776. By March of that Spring, the "big guns" were firmly in place overlooking Boston harbor from Dorchester Heights. This very successful defensive measure by the Continental Army caused Commander William Howe to withdraw all British troops to Halifax, Nova Scotia on March 17th, celebrated as *Evacuation Day*!
Although a strong leader and motivator of men, many battles would follow under Washington's leadership that brought defeat to the Colonial Army. Not a brilliant military strategist at first, Washington often found himself with poorly trained, poorly clothed and under-fed troops. Nonetheless, the Continental Army would hold its own against the British tyrants.

America Declares Its Independence

As fighting continued on several fronts, the Second Continental Congress debated on in Philadelphia. Twelve of the 13 American colonies had sent delegates. It wasn't until a year later that Georgia eventually sent delegates on July 20th of 1775. Although the Continental Congress had no official authority to act, it began to act as a quasi-government body, appointing ambassadors, signing treaties and making its own paper money known as "Continentals".

Although many of the delegates from the original 13 colonies were proposing independence from the British Crown, others were reluctant. Those who advocated independence encouraged some colonies to replace their colonial governments and send new delegates to the Second Congress. In May of 1776, the Congress passed a very important regulation which recommended that all 13 colonies should adopt pro-independence legislatures if they were not already so.

Then, on June 7, 1776 the Congress adopted a Resolution of Independence which not only declared independence from Britain but also laid the groundwork for beneficial foreign alliances and treaties. The Congress then passed the official *United States Declaration of Independence* on July 4th, 1776!

Assembly room in Philadelphia's Independence Hall where the Declaration of Independence was passed on July 4, 1776

Due to growing fear that the British would attempt to capture members of the Second Continental Congress in Philadelphia, the Congress was moved to Baltimore in the winter of 1776, then eventually to York, Pennsylvania in September of 1777.

Following initial success in the *Siege of Boston*, Washington and his troops marched on to New York City where British General William Howe had amassed a rather sizeable force of 32,000 soldiers, including 9,000 German recruits from the German state of Hesse, thus the title "Hessian mercenaries". It was August of 1776, and George Washington was now 44 years of age.

Washington had located his men on the tip of Manhattan and across the East River in what Brooklyn Heights. In what is considered one of Washington's poorer decisions, he decided to leave his left flank unprotected, allowing Howe and his British troops to pour in behind the colonial's front lines, essentially separating the American forces.

In a futile attempt to strengthen his now-weak position on Manhattan, Washington brought three additional regiments across the East River. At this point Howe could have heavily harmed the colonial troops but as he waited from his brother, Admiral Richard Howe, to direct his fleet of ships to launch an artillery barrage, the weather became too challenging for the ships to maneuver and to begin the onslaught. Washington, in a change of heart, realized that the American cause was futile and quickly evacuated 9,500 militia back across the East River to Manhattan.

Rather than launch an all-out assault on Manhattan, Admiral Richard Howe committed a strategic error in sailing his soldiers further up the East River to gain what he thought was an advantage. Instead, his move allowed Washington time to order his troops out of the city, out of reach of the British army, and into eastern Pennsylvania. Although colonial troops had escaped certain disaster, the death toll was over, 800 were wounded and over 1,000 taken prisoner. But in spite of such severe losses, the Continental Army lived to fight another day. And fight they would!

With winter coming fast, British troops chose to winter over in Trenton and Princeton, New Jersey, just south of New York City. This decision would set the stage for two of the war's pivotal battles, the *Battles of Trenton and Princeton*, beginning on the evening of Christmas Day, 1776.

The town of Trenton, New jersey was under the control of a relatively small British force of approximately 1,400 Hessian soldiers under the leadership of Colonel Johann Rall. Washington and the Continental Army, consisting of approximately 2,400 militiamen, hoped to take the town through the element of surprise. The great risk, obviously, was crossing the very icy and dangerous Delaware River under the cloak of darkness in small boats. Washington's strategy was to attack with two separate divisions of militia from the northwest and to bring two additional divisions through the south side of Trenton. Unfortunately, only two of the four planned divisions were able to cross the treacherous waters, leaving Major General Nathaniel Greene and Major General John Sullivan on their own to take on the British.

It was hoped, and rumored later, that the British might still be drunk or hung over from too much Christmas celebration. Instead, the successful takeover of Trenton and capture of hundreds of Hessians would be attributed to the timing of a classic Nor'easter (howling snowstorm) rather than holiday cheer!

The noise of the storm drowned out the sound of approaching colonial soldiers, likely weary and wet from their dangerous river crossing. The success of the attack can also be attributed to the brilliant and effective use of colonial sympathizer, John Honeymoon, enlisted as a spy by General Washington to determine the size of the Hessian army as well as to mislead the Hessians about the strength and intentions of the American militia. The

Hessians had also failed to send out their normal nightly scouting patrols due to the intense storm.

Due to a long 6-hour delay in the arrival of the Continental Army at McConkey's Ferry crossing, American troops did not cross the Delaware until 4:00 a.m. Once across, troops began their 9-mile March to Trenton, where the battle commenced at about 8:00 a.m. Miraculously, this all-important battle was over within an hour.

Trivial Fun Fact

The popular painting of *Washington Crossing the Delaware*, by Emanuel Leutze, is more about symbolism than reality. The crossing, as recorded, occurred during freezing rain and driving snow, well before sunrise! Washington would have likely been seated under such conditions. Now you know!

At battle's end, following several skirmishes throughout the city and cannon volleys by the American rebels, 23 Hessians lie dead, including Colonel Johann Rall. Over 900 Hessians were taken captive. The Americans suffered only a handful of wounded. Sadly, two American soldiers died from hypothermia during the march to Trenton. Others died from the cold the next evening.

Washington's troops, along with hundreds of Hessian prisoners and captured supplies, crossed back into Pennsylvania by noon. Imagine the physical toll of marching 9 miles to engage in a battle, then marching 9 miles back to the ferry crossing and then further into Pennsylvania, following the physical conflict.

The adrenaline must have been running high as the Continental Army had now proven itself battle-worthy in conquering a well-organized Hessian army of several battalions. The *Battles of Trenton and Princeton* would also prove critical in luring additional colonial militia into the ranks of the Continental Army as the American rebels gained a sense of being able to win the conflict over the British and the well-trained Hessian troops.

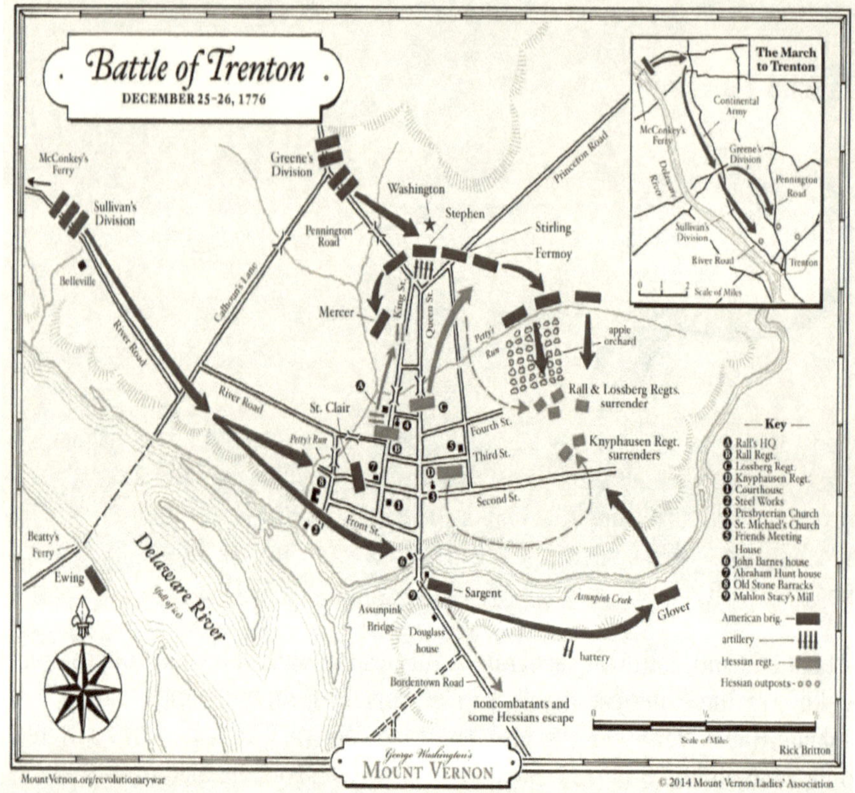

Battle of Trenton
DECEMBER 25–26, 1776

Trivial Fun Fact

One of the two wounded soldiers at *The Battle of Trenton* was future president and young lieutenant, James Monroe. Dr. John Riker saved his life by clamping an artery in his shoulder, which had been severed by a musket ball. Now you know!

Then just a week later, on January 3, 1777, Washington decided to engineer a surprise attack on the 1,400 British troops wintering over in Princeton, New Jersey. Turning toward Princeton, Washington's forces once again passed through Trenton where they encountered a British force on the eve of January 2nd. Washington held off at least three separate skirmishes provoked by British troops. Casualty reports vary widely from very few killed or wounded on either side to over a 100 killed or wounded on each side.

This minor but strategic victory for the American forces is known as *The Battle of Assunpink Creek* and *The Second Battle of Trenton*. British forces were forced to retreat from New Jersey for the Winter of 1777.

The next morning, at 2 a.m. on January 3, 1777, Washington marched his troops north to Princeton with a force that had grown to between 5,000 and 6,000 as several hundred untrained militiamen joined the Continental Army. Meanwhile British General Cornwallis was on the main road to Trenton with 8,000 Redcoats with the intentions of destroying the Continental Army. Washington decided to march quietly past the British, down a back road and through a private farm to Princeton, which the British army failed to guard that evening, thereby avoiding the larger British force. When Washington's troops arrived in Princeton, they met a sparse rear guard of British soldiers which they outnumbered 5 to 1. The ensuing battle claimed 40 patriots and 275 British soldiers. More importantly, this decisive defeat forced brothers William and Richard Howe to flea New Jersey for the North Atlantic coast!

In response to Washington's impressive victories at Trenton and Princeton, the British response was, once again, an attempt to destroy the rebel militia once and for all. British General William Howe had regrouped and developed a strategy to capture various colonialcontrolled business and political centers. Howe set his sights first on Philadelphia, with a plan to attack there in the summer of 1777.

Once Howe's plan was learned by the American rebels, Washington and his troops relocated to defend *The City of Brotherly Love*. Howe departed New York City in July of 1777, 16,000 troops strong! Meanwhile, the Continental Army had grown to a force of 15,000, setting the stage for a potentially large conflict. After weeks of maneuvering and planning, the British army moved upon the city of Philadelphia on September 11, 1777, where they would be required to cross Brandywine Creek at various points called fords. General William Howe advanced under the pretense that the hundreds of British loyalists already living in Philadelphia would rise up against the Continental Army.

General Charles Cornwallis was in charge of one British regiment of 9,000 while Lieutenant General Wilhelm von Knyphausen lead a second force of 7,000 men. Although Washington's troops had blocked what he thought were the northern-most (Wistar) and southernmost fords (Pyle). Washington had strategically located his artillery on high ground at a halfway point between Wistar and Pyle Fords with the hope of engaging Howe's troops somewhere in this middle ground near Chadds Ford. Relying on Loyalist scouting reports, Howe learned of an unblocked ford north of Wistar,

Trivial Fun Fact

Not all of the colonists were sympathetic to the rebel cause and did not support the efforts of the Continental Army. There were some estimates that as many as 60% of British colonials were conservatives who remained loyal to the King. Those who remained loyal to Great Britain were referred to as Tories, Loyalists, King's Men, and Royalists. Now you know!

where he and his troops were able to cross without incident, surprising Washington's unguarded north flank.

Although an intense battle did occur early in the morning between Knyphausen's troops and the Continental Army at Chadds Ford, Cornwallis' regiment of 9,000 strong was proceeding on an exhausting 9-hour march upon Washington's unguarded flank. Washington disregarded early scouting reports about a second British advance, learning too late that his unguarded flank was in serious danger.

The second British attack began around 4 p.m. on the afternoon of September 11th. Unable to assemble a suitable defense following intense battle conditions, the Continental Army was forced to leave behind valuable cannons as they went into full retreat. The ferocious battle ended at sundown with Howe's men too tired to continue pursuit of the retreating Americans. Although a clear victory for the British troops, who captured the battlefield at Brandywine Creek on that day, Washington's army escaped, weakened but not destroyed, able to return to Philadelphia.

British casualties at Brandywine totaled 80 to 90 dead, and 488 wounded while the Americans lost 200-300 fighters with nearly 600 more wounded and 400 captured. It would not be until two weeks later, on September 26th that the British overtook Philadelphia. Meanwhile the Second Continental Congress had rescued time to remove important military information and supplies from their capital.

On a second battle front, British forces once again lead by General John Burgoyne attempted to sever colonial New England from the rest of the colonies in an attack staged against colonial forces along the eastern state line of New York at Schuylerville.

It was here, at the *Battles of Saratoga*, on September 19th and October 7th that Burgoyne suffered two stinging defeats at the hands of colonial forces, losing over 1,000 troops while the colonials listed 500 as lost or wounded.

Trivial Fun Fact

In his efforts to properly defend Saratoga in August of 1777, General George

Washington recruited 500 of his top shooters from Maryland, Pennsylvania, and Virginia. This group of highly-skilled marksmen were named the *Provisional Rifle Corps* and were placed under the leadership of Colonel Daniel Morgan. This very valuable unit became known as *Morgan's Riflemen.* Now you know!

Most importantly, the outcome at the *Battles of Saratoga* compelled France and Spain to join the conflict on the side of the Americans.

Meanwhile, on October 4th, Washington battled British one more time prior to setting up winter quarters. Just outside of Philadelphia, British General William Howe had moved 9,000 of his 12,000 men to Germantown to provide ongoing protection for the city of Philadelphia.

Washington thought he once again had an opportunity to surprises Howe as he entered the battle in position of strength with 11,000 men. But a series of communication breakdowns, along with foggy conditions, eventually resulted in a second major British victory and the loss or capture of nearly 1,100 American militiamen. The British suffered over 500 killed or wounded.

Failing to retake Philadelphia, Washington and his remaining 12,000 militiamen retreated 18 miles to the northwest of the American capital city where they would winter over at Valley Forge.

The Germantown Battle became fierce at Cliveden, home of Benjamin Chew
(Public Domain and PinIt)

A French Alliance on the Horizon

Valley Forge was the Continental Army's first major attempt at building an encampment. Perched on high ground between two small mountains, the camp was strategically located near to the Schuylkill River and in close proximity to Philadelphia, with the possibility that Washington's militia might advance on the capital city during the winter.

Historians estimate that between 1,300 and 1,600 individual small log cabins were built to house Washington's men. The huts were roofed in grass thatch, boards, and branches. The river provided a necessary supply route while the open fields allowed for training and marching.

The winter of 1777 at Valley Forge looked as if it might signal the beginning of the end for the sometimes valiant, but recently defeated, Continental Army. As deadly as the warfare itself, Washington's beleaguered and battle-weary troops would experience hunger, disease, and desertion beyond imagination. It is estimated that between 1,700 and 2,000 men were lost to disease and malnutrition! Nearly 1,500 horses also died from starvation. Washington himself was distraught to the point of stating, "If the army does not get help soon, in all likelihood it will disband".

Trivial Fun Fact

Shortly after setting up camp at Valley Forge on December 19, of 1777, there was an immediate shortage of food supplies. Many of Washington's soldiers survived on "firecake", a bland blend of water and flour which they cooked upon the rocks surrounding their campfires. Now you know!

A limited supply of both food and clothing was a chronic problem in that challenging winter of 1777-1778. Main food staples included salted beef, fish, and pork along with flour, bread, and a "gill" of whiskey daily, which is half a cup or 4 ounces. Many men also did not have coats and boots.

It was recorded in the diary of an Irish immigrant, Christopher Marshall, that on January 9th, 1778 loyal female supporters from Philadelphia marched "ten teams of oxen, fit for slaughter" into the encampment and delivered 200 shirts sown by rebel sympathizers in Philadelphia.

In spite of the brutal winter and staggering losses, his prayer would eventually be answered. As the weather eased toward February and March, the Continental Army was blessed by the appointment of General Nathaniel Greene, who was placed in charge of rations and supplies. Magically, food and clothing began to appear in goodly amounts, although later than needed.

Equally encouraging was the work of the German mercenary, Baron von Steuben, who began to transform untrained recruits into capable fighters on the plains outside of the Valley Forge encampment.

A close friend of Washington, Alexander Hamilton and Thomas Jefferson was Major General Marquis de Lafayette, a French officer who was wounded at Brandywine, would become instrumental in gaining support from his native country. He had come to the United States at the young age of 19. In May, France pledged both money and other resources to the Colonial effort.

After returning to his homeland to lobby for even more financial resources for the American effort, Lafayette returned in 1780 when he was assigned a greater leadership role in the Continental Army. By June of 1778, the Continental Army had returned to fighting form and set its sights on Philadelphia and New Jersey!

Trivial Fun Fact

Major General Marquis de Lafayette, born of a wealthy aristocratic French family, was commissioned as an officer in the French Army at the age of 13.

Generals Washington and Lafayette at Valley Forge Copyright 1807, by Brown and Bigelow

Philadelphia and Beyond

British General William Howe had been replaced by Lieutenant General Sir Henry Clinton in the Spring of 1778 with orders to abandon the city for New York, where the French were threatening a blockade. The British were also required to send troops to the West Indies to defend their interests there. With as many as 20,000 British troop now in Philadelphia as well as a few hundred British loyalists, the immense evacuation would not be easy.

On June 18th, Washington immediately assigned Major General Benedict Arnold to serve as temporary commander over the city, with the Continental Congress returning shortly thereafter.

Learning that the majority of Clinton's armies were returning to New York on foot, lacking enough ships to transport thousands of British troops by river, Washington put his army in quick pursuit. On June 28th, Washington and his militia came upon Clinton's forces at Monmouth, New Jersey, where 25,000 combined forces would do battle!

After intense fighting on a blistering, 96-degree day, neither party emerged with a clear victory, with both armies suffering between 300 and 500 killed or wounded. It has been reported that nearly as many men may have died from heat exhaustion as musket fire.

Nightfall eventually brought the battle to an end. Although there was no clear victory for the Colonials, Clinton's undetected nighttime departure for New York City was telling. The Continental Army had demonstrated its effectiveness, improved discipline and fighting skills under von Steuben and Lafayette, in holding off a larger British force.

Washington Rallying the Troops at Monmouth Emanuel Leutze – Public Domain

The Battle of Monmouth would be that final battle which engaged both of the large, main armies. Action would shift to the southern colonies where French troops would play a greater role in important battles. Lafayette had returned to France where he asked King Louis XVI for additional resources to aid the American colonists. King Louis responded with the aid of several hundred ground forces under Count de Rochambeau.

Washington and Lafayette teamed up again at Morristown, New Jersey, as the American traitor, Benedict Arnold, was laying plans to deceive his own colonial troops and leaders. Although Arnold escaped to Europe before he could be brought to justice, his accomplice, Major John Andre, was caught and hanged for treason.

While Rochambeau and French forces were sailing to America, the British turned their efforts to the southern colonies, capturing Charleston, South Carolina in May of 1780.The colonists eventually turned the tide under Nathanael Greene. British leader, Lord Cornwallis, developed a plan to defeat a smaller colonial force under Lafayette at Yorktown on the Virginia coast.

Learning of Cornwallis' plan, Washington immediately re-directed his land forces and ordered French ground troops and the French fleet to march and ail upon Yorktown in attempt to surprise Cornwallis' troops. Trapped by land and blockaded by sea, Cornwallis had little choice but to surrender his 8,000 troops on October 17, 1781! The last British troops remaining in the colonies departed Sandy Hook, New Jersey and New York City in September of 1783 with the signing of the treaty.

What does the Treaty of Paris mean?

- 10 Main Articles in the Treaty of Paris
  - 1: 13 colonies are free and can govern themselves
  - 2: Boundaries established with U.S. and Britain
  - 3: Fishing rights granted to U.S.
  - 4: Debts acknowledged to be paid
  - 5: Congress of Confederation gives loyalists land
  - 6: U.S. prevents future conflicts with loyalists
  - 7: War prisoners released and British property now U.S.
  - 8: Britain and U.S. given access to Mississippi River
  - 9: Land captured to be returned
  - 10: Certification of the Treaty occur in 6 months

Washington Returns to Mt. Vernon

Yorktown, Virginia   October 19, 1781

YORKTOWN IS WON!

Cornwallis' Sword is Delivered to American Forces

"The World Turned Upside Down"

Although the Revolutionary War would not officially end for two years with the *Treaty of Paris*, the American victory at *Yorktown* marked an unofficial end to the first American civil war. Much of the French military force had departed the colonies by 1782, but most of Washington's loyal soldiers had not been paid for several years because the Continental treasury was broke!

Washington urged Congress, in March of 1783, to approve a bill rewarding former militiamen with a fiveyear bonus for their service. Then, he said good bye to his troops on December 23, 1783, nearly 8 ½ years after being named Commanding General of the Continental Army!

Although Washington was still relatively young at the end of the war at just 51 years of age, he had experienced more than most men in their lifetimes. But how easy would it be to return to the life of a gentleman farmer, a second time? Recall that he first retired 24 years earlier to Mt. Vernon (1759), following the French and Indian War.

Trivial Fun Fact

George Washington first fell in love at the age of 16 with Sally Fairfax, who was married at the time. Although their friendship continued into adulthood, they never married. George expressed his love for Sally in his personal diary through a poem. Now you know!

"Going home" for Washington meant returning to a very large and demanding agricultural operation. He and Martha had amassed over 8,000 acres with 5 fully-operational farms. Washington also bought and sold tens of thousands of acres as far west as West Virginia and Ohio, along the Ohio and Kanawha Rivers.

His farming endeavors included a large variety of livestock; horses, goats, pigs, guinea hens, prize bulls, rams, and sheep. As a planter, Washington practiced crop rotation and unique plowing methods in order to preserve the nutritional value of his land. He eventually abandoned tobacco growing as it was very hard on the land. He developed a grist mill and distillery along with a large fishery.

In order to feed over 300 slaves, his farms also produced very large fields of carrots, cabbage, potatoes, peas, beans, pumpkins, and turnips. His vast fruit orchards included apples, cherries, pears, apricots, peaches, and plums.

Although it could be argued that through his efforts to make his farms and slave labor as effective as possible, Washington pursued his own self-interests. But, the positive outcomes achieved at Mt. Vernon were clearly beneficial to the agricultural industry. What was good for Mt. Vernon was also good for America! And although he and Martha built a personal agricultural empire in their day, George Washington sacrificed many of his adult years and risked his life in countless battles to preserve the new nation.

It would take only 4 short years for Washington to once again hear the call to leadership, a role that could not escape him. The young nation continued to tread on an insecure footing under the Articles of Confederation. Although written between 1776 and 1777 by the Second Continental Congress, the Articles were not ratified by all 13 colonies until March of 1781.

It soon became apparent that in an effort to preserve the sovereignty and power of the separate 13 colonies, the new central government, the Congress of the Confederation, or Continental Congress, as it was better know, proved too weak to address bigger mutual concerns and threats.

In 1787, war veteran Daniel Shays, along with 4,000 of his recruits staged a rebellion in Springfield, Massachusetts in protest of perceived economic and civil rights injustices. *Shays Rebellion*, as history would recall the event, ended in a failed attempt to capture the United States Armory at Springfield. The rebels suffered 4 killed while the Continental Army had but one casualty. Dozens of men on both sides were injured, and two rebels were later hanged. Protests in northern Massachusetts had begun as early as 1782, primarily to prevent colonial tax- collectors from doing their work.
When Governor James Bowdoin replaced Massachusetts Governor Hancock in 1785, he immediately renewed efforts to collect back taxes as the colonial legislature passed a property tax bill to pay of the American colony's debts to foreign nations. This as a time when very few New England farmers owned little more than their land and livestock. John Adams remarked as this time, that the situation had become far too much for the new colonials to handle.

Amidst the cries of a suffering colonial nation, George Washington once again answered the call to leadership, as the Continental Congress, in 1786, approved a convention to amend the Articles of the Confederation in Philadelphia.

When George Washingto was only 14, he attempted to join the British Army, which would have required him to go away to sea. We are thankful to George's Mother, Mary Ball, for denying him that opportunity at such a young age. Now you know!

A President is Chosen . . . A Constitution is Ratified

In the company of such patriots as Alexander Hamilton and James Madison, George Washington joined the movement to not simply amend the Articles of Confederation, but to replace them with a stronger document for all time! The task would not be easy. A strong central government plan was opposed by patriots, Sam Adams and Patrick Henry, who feared Washington's efforts were an attempt to weaken the colonies. Despite ongoing protest, the *US Constitution* was ratified in a close vote in 1788.

Under the newly-established electoral college, Washington received a vote from every single elector of the College, the only president in US history to receive unanimous approval as well as the only president in US history who did not have to campaign prior to the election!

Although he first declined the established annual salary of $25,000, Washington later accepted so that Congress would not give the impression that only wealthy men or women could serve as president.

First Page of the US Constitution
Ratified June 21, 1788 (Wikipedia)

Although he did not belong to any political party . . . they did not yet exist . . . Washington favored a strong federal government. His preference appears to make sense in light of the previous five years of colonial rebellion following the Revolutionary War. This idea of a strong national government would be promoted by Alexander Hamilton and the newly-formed Federalist Party.

The President's House in Philadelphia
was Washington's official residence from 1790 to 1797

Opposed to this arrangement was Thomas Jefferson, who would later form the Jeffersonian Republican party. It is said that Washington nearly dismissed Jefferson as his Secretary of State due to his opposition to Hamilton's ideas. Interestingly enough, the Federalist and Jeffersonian Republican parties represent the early roots of today's modern day Democratic and Republican parties. Over 200 years later, the debate goes on over whether America is stronger with big federal government or whether our fundamental rights should be decided within each state.

Although Washington never joined the Federalist party, he promoted a strong national bank and federal taxing system. He is also remembered for avoiding foreign wars, creation of the President's cabinet of department heads, the inaugural address, and his insistence on being called *Mr. President* rather wear a title of nobility or royalty. Washington's two-term

Trivial Fun Fact

The 22nd amendment to the US constitution was ratified by three-fourths of the states in February of 1951, which limited the presidency to two elected terms. Now you know!

presidency became a tradition that lasted until 1940, when Franklin Delano Roosevelt was elected to a third term and, finally, a fourth term in 1944! Interestingly enough, many presidential scholars today rank the three greatest presidents of all time as George Washington, Abraham Lincoln, and Franklin D. Roosevelt.

It is also said that Washington proved to be a good judge of character and talent. He would listen to opposing opinions but would act decisively once he had listened. He feared the formation of a two-party system that could harm the republic through excessive conflict and in-fighting. Refusing to be considered for a third term, in September of 1796, Washington authored and delivered the first Farewell Address in the form of a letter to the public

It was in his departing letter that Washington warned of the dangers of factionalism and regional fighting to the new republic. He also warned of the risk of a strong central government taking power from the people and entrusting it to unjust power-hungry government leaders. Finally, it was Washington's hope that the checks and balances that were built into the new Constitution would ensure the strength of the new nation. He felt that change should come through Constitutional amendment, not through force or anarchy.

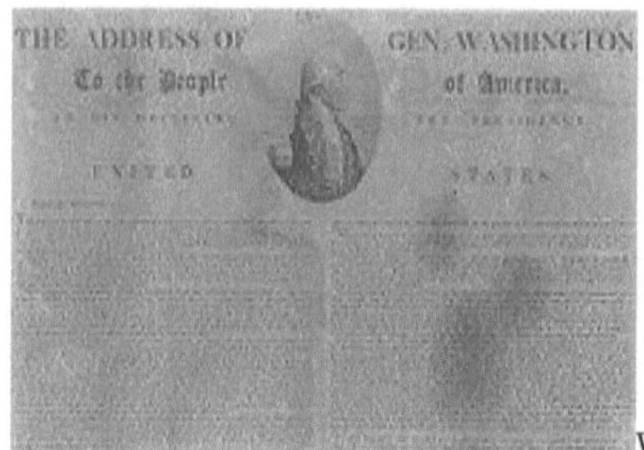

Washington's Farewell Address, September 1796

Washington's Final Return to Mt. Vernon

With perhaps more resolve and peace of mind than he felt following the Revolutionary War, Washington packed up his belongings and returned once again to his beloved Mt. Vernon in the Spring of 1797. In Washington's absence, many of the plantation operations were witnessing little profit, although Washington had great wealth in land and slaves. It is estimated that Mt. Vernon's worth exceeded $1 million in 1799, the equivalent of nearly $20 million in 2014.

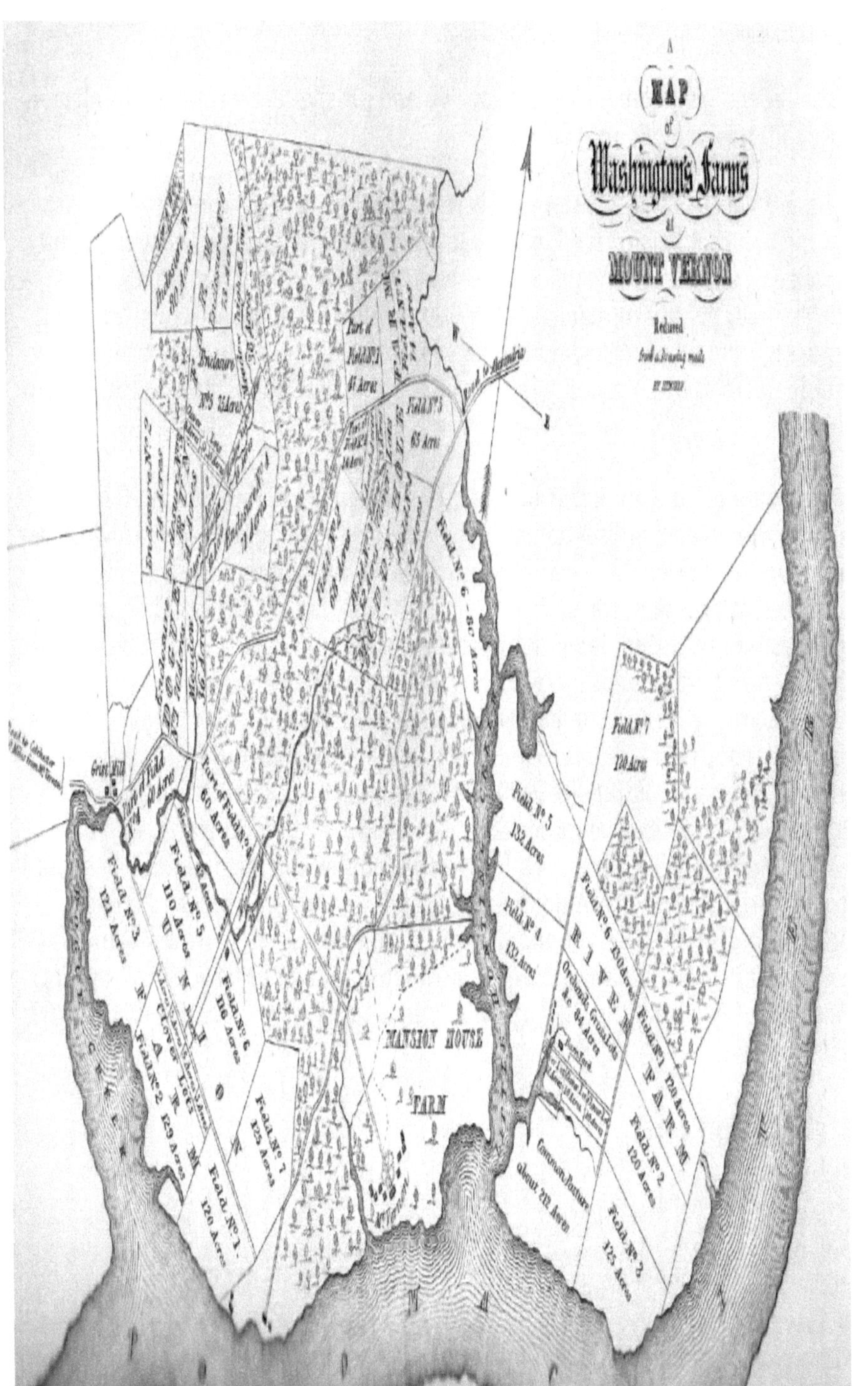

A
MAP
of
Washington's Farms
at
MOUNT VERNON
Reduced
from a Drawing made
BY HIMSELF
Road to Alexandria
N
S
Grist Mill
Field No 1
Field No 2
Field No 3
Field No 5
Part of Field No 3
Part of Field No 4
Field No 6
Field No 5
Field No 4
Field No 6
Field No 7
MANSION HOUSE
FARM
RIVER FARM
Common Pasture
Orchard Garden
Field No 1
Field No 2
Field No 3

The Plantations of Mt. Vernon, 1799 (Wikipedia)

The federal government would survive and prosper under the newly-elected second president, John Adams.

If there was irony in Washington's remarkably full and productive life, it was in the fact that he survived many battles through two major wars, efficiently managed department heads, helped launch a new nation, but struggled throughout his life to manage his 8,000 acre personal estate, consisting of five separate farms. Washington had spent most of his adult life trying to settle down at Mt. Vernon, where he had lived off and on since three years of age!

According to an eyewitness account, on December 12th, 1799, at 10 a.m., nearly three years after leaving the presidency, Washington went to work his property on horseback when he was caught in rain, wind, and hail. He returned after 3 p.m. for dinner, noticeably wet, but he did not change his clothes before sitting down to dinner. Showing no signs of illness he went to bed as usual after his daily review of the mail. He awoke the next morning with a sore throat and some hoarseness. Nonetheless, he once again rode his horse out onto the plantation to mark some trees for removal.
He awoke at approximately 3:00 a.m. with great difficulty breathing and speaking. Following the rather normal procedure of bloodletting, one of Washington's three physicians recommended that his team of doctors should perform a tracheotomy which would open Washington's blocked airway. With two of three doctors unfamiliar with this relatively new procedure, which could have possibly saved Washington's life, a tracheotomy was not performed. Washington died at 10:00 p.m. that evening, December 14, 1799. He was 67.

Trivial Fun Fact

George Washington's official cause of death is agreed by many medical experts to likely have been *bacterial epiglottitis*, an inflammation of the epiglottis, which would have blocked air into the lungs. Now you know!

A funeral was held four days later on December 18th and Washington was buried at Mt. Vernon. Napoleon Bonaparte ordered 10 days of mourning in France and ships of the British Royal Navy Channel Fleet lowered their flags to half-mast.

The Washington Monument in Washington D.C. (Wikipedia)

America's first president has been memorialized and honored through many monuments, a national holiday, a Mt. Rushmore bust, countless U.S. postage stamps, the U.S. one dollar bill, and the U.S. quarter, just to name a few. I believe a comment by one of his fellow Revolutionary War comrades best summarizes Washington's awesome life!

Henry "Light-Horse Harry" Lee read the following eulogy for General

Washington following his death: "First in war - first in peace - and first in the hearts of his countrymen".
THE END

Memorials to George Washington

Bailly's George Washington, Independence Hall, Philadelphia, Pennsylvania
(Smallbones - Own work, CC0,

The first Washington Monument in Baltimore, Maryland
(DavoP - Own work, CC BY-SA 3.0,

GEORGE WASHINGTON
The General Assembly of the Commonwealth of
Virginia have caused this Statue to be erected
as a monument of affection and gratitude to
GEORGE WASHINGTON

Jean-Antoine Houdon's statue, State Capitol in Virginia
(User:AlbertHerring - Image taken by me for Wikipedia, CC BY 3.0,

The equestrian sculpture of George Washington at the center of Washington Circle, a traffic circle and public park, located on the
boundary of the Foggy Bottom and West End neighborhoods in Washington, D.C.

(By AgnosticPreachersKid - Own work, CC BY-SA 3.0,